HIP HOP VIOLA

Etudes, Patterns & Licks

(2nd Edition)

HARRY HUNT, JR., MFA

Hip Hop Viola Etudes, Patterns, & Licks
Harry Hunt, Jr., MFA

©2025 Harry Hunt, Jr.

All Rights Reserved. No part of this book may be reproduced in any form without written permission from the publisher.

Published by A2G Entertainment Inc.

ISBN: 978-1-954127-40-1 (paperback)

Printed in the USA
Second Edition

ABOUT THE AUTHOR

Harry Hunt, Jr. "The Modern Violinist" is a versatile violinist who has successfully connected the worlds of classical and contemporary music. His journey began with intensive classical training, mastering works from Bach to Tchaikovsky, driven by a deep passion for exploring different musical styles. During his college years at Ohio State University, where he earned his bachelor's degree in jazz studies, Harry took an unexpected turn, immersing himself in jazz guitar and piano studies—a decision that would ultimately reshape his approach to the violin. He later furthered his education at Columbia College Chicago, earning a Master of Fine Arts degree in composition.

This diverse musical foundation led to a dynamic career spanning multiple instruments and genres. For over a decade, Harry toured internationally as a pianist, guitarist, and bassist with R&B, soul, and gospel acts before returning to his first love—the violin. Through this unique path, he developed an innovative approach to string playing that combines classical precision with the soulful expression of contemporary genres.

Harry has performed and recorded with renowned artists including Chance the Rapper, Tony! Toni! Tone!, Chaka Khan, and Lauryn Hill. As an educator and innovator, his mission is to empower classical string players to find their authentic voice in modern music. Drawing from his three decades of experience, Harry has developed a comprehensive system that transforms traditionally trained violinists into versatile musicians capable of playing by ear, improvising, and performing authentically in any style.

CONTENTS

Play-Along Backing Tracks	1
Introduction	3
The Amplified Viola	4
A Minor	**6**
Melodic Minor Scale	7
Harmonic Minor Scale	8
Arpeggios (Quarters)	9
Arpeggios (8ths)	10
Popular Classical Licks	11
8th Note Licks	15
16th Note Licks	17
D Minor	**20**
Melodic Minor Scale	21
Harmonic Minor Scale	22
Arpeggios (Quarters)	23
Arpeggios (8ths)	24
Popular Classical Licks	25
8th Note Licks	29
16th Note Licks	31
G Minor	**34**
Melodic Minor Scale	35
Harmonic Minor Scale	36
Arpeggios (Quarters)	37
Arpeggios (8ths)	38
Popular Classical Licks	39
8th Note Licks	43
16th Note Licks	45
C Minor	**48**
Melodic Minor Scale	49
Harmonic Minor Scale	50
Arpeggios (Quarters)	51
Arpeggios (8ths)	52
Popular Classical Licks	53
8th Note Licks	57
16th Note Licks	59

PLAY-ALONG BACKING TRACKS

To Stream or Download
Click or Visit
harryhuntjr.net/book-easyhiphoplicks

OTHER LINKS

https://sites.google.com/view/book-tracks/viola

(bookmark links in your browser for quicker access)

©2025 Harry Hunt, Jr.

Using Your Backing Tracks

Included with your "Hip Hop Viola: Etudes, Patterns and Licks" book are backing tracks that transform your practice into an interactive musical experience.

What You'll Find

Backing Tracks: Play along with professional hip hop beats and accompaniment that create an authentic experience. These tracks give you the freedom to experiment with the techniques, patterns, and licks you're learning.

Making the Most of Your Tracks

1. Follow Along: Use the backing tracks while practicing the etudes and patterns in your book.

2. Get Creative: Once you're comfortable with the written exercises, try:
   - Changing rhythms while using the same notes
   - Starting patterns on different beats of the measure
   - Creating your own licks using techniques from the book
   - Experimenting with different bow and pizzicato techniques

3. Build Your Timing: The backing tracks provide the essential hip hop groove and beat that helps develop your sense of rhythm and flow.

4. Extend Your Practice: These tracks make practice more engaging, which means you'll practice longer and more often!

Remember, these backing tracks aren't just beats – they're teaching tools designed to help you develop an authentic hip hop feel while making practice something you actually look forward to!

INTRODUCTION

Introduction: Getting Started
Are you a violist who wants to play hip hop? This book is for you! While hip hop might seem simple, there are so many ways you can create your own sound with your viola.

In this book, you'll find classical melodies and 16th note patterns that will give you new ideas for your next hip hop performance. These exercises will help whether you've only played classical music before or you're already trying out hip hop sounds.

Don't Just Read the Music
Hip hop is all about expressing yourself, not just reading notes on a page. The patterns in this book are starting points to help you create your own style. Your goal should be to learn the music and then play it without looking at the page.

Try each exercise with the backing track until you can play it from memory. Then, try changing it up - make your own versions by adding different rhythms or notes. One cool trick is to play everything twice as fast: turn 8th notes into 16th notes or quarter notes into 8th notes. This makes the exercises more challenging and helps you come up with new ideas.

Start with a Metronome
If the play-along tracks are too fast at first, use a metronome instead. Set it to a speed that's comfortable for you, then slowly increase the tempo until you can keep up with the play-along tracks. This step-by-step approach helps build both your speed and your timing.

Remember: in hip hop viola, having good rhythm is just as important as playing the right notes. Find your own style and use these patterns to create your unique hip hop viola sound.

Time to pick up your viola and make some music!

THE AMPLIFIED VIOLA

Hey there! Ready to make your viola sound awesome for hip hop? Before we get into the cool patterns and licks, let's talk about making your viola loud enough to be heard alongside beats, bass, and other hip hop elements. Don't worry - it's not as complicated as it might seem!

What You'll Need

1. Choose Your Instrument
- *Acoustic Viola:* with pickup
- *Electric Viola:* already built for amplification and effects

*If using your regular viola, you'll need a **pickup**:*
- Fishman V-200V
- The Realist Viola Pickup

If using an electric viola:
- Pickup already built in
- Many have volume and tone controls right on the viola
- Some have effects built in (like reverb)

2. A Preamp
- Makes your viola's signal stronger and clearer
- Helps shape your tone
- Good Option: LR Baggs ParaAcoustic DI
- Budget Option: Behringer V-Tone Acoustic Driver DI
- (Many electric violas have this built in)

3. An Amplifier or PA System
- At least 50 watts of power
- Built-in effects (especially reverb)
- A way to connect to bigger sound systems

4. Effects Pedals (Optional but Fun!)
- Looper: Record short patterns to play over
- Delay: Create echo effects
- Distortion: For a gritty, urban sound
- Octave: Add bass notes below your playing

Setting Everything Up

1. Connect in this order:
- *Viola → Pickup → Preamp → Effects (if any) → Amp/PA*

2. Adjusting Your Sound for Hip Hop:
- Boost the mid-range to cut through beats
- Use less reverb than you would for jazz

Common Problems and Quick Fixes

Sound Too Quiet?
- Check all your connections
- Make sure your preamp is on and batteries are fresh

Getting Feedback (that high-pitched squeal)?
- Move away from speakers
- Turn down volume

Remember: Keep things simple at first! Focus on getting a clean, strong sound before worrying about fancy effects. The most important thing is that your viola playing shines through, even with all the technology.

Now that you know how to be heard, let's move on to some awesome hip hop patterns and licks!

A MINOR

MELODIC MINOR SCALE
A MINOR

HARMONIC MINOR SCALE
A MINOR

ARPEGGIOS (QUARTERS)
A MINOR

1

2

3

4

ARPEGGIOS (8ths)
A MINOR

1

2

3

4

5

©2025 Harry Hunt, Jr.

POPULAR CLASSICAL LICKS
A MINOR

Mouret: Rondeau

Mozart: The Marriage of Figaro

Grieg: In the Hall of the Mountain King

Bach: Little Fugue #1

©2025 Harry Hunt, Jr.

Mozart: Eine Kleine

9

Bach: Little Fugue #2

10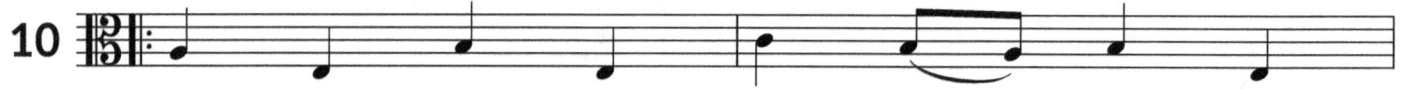

Bach: Suite #2

11

Tchaikovsky: 1812 Overture

12

Bizet: Carmen (Overture)

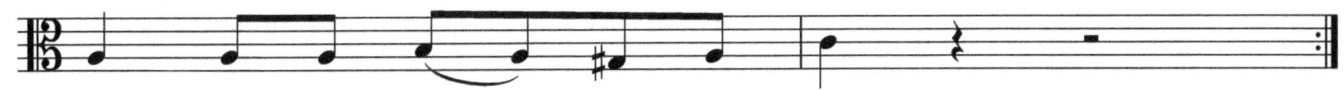

Bizet: Carmen (Habanera)

Bach: Jesu, Joy of Man's Desiring

Mozart: Rondo Alla Turca

©2025 Harry Hunt, Jr.

8th NOTE LICKS
A MINOR

1

2

3

4

5

6

7

8

9

10

16th NOTE LICKS
A MINOR

1

2

3

4

5

6

7

8

9

10

©2025 Harry Hunt, Jr.

D MINOR

MELODIC MINOR SCALE
D MINOR

HARMONIC MINOR SCALE
D MINOR

ARPEGGIOS (QUARTERS)
D MINOR

1

2

3

4

ARPEGGIOS (8ths)
D MINOR

1

2

3

4

5

POPULAR CLASSICAL LICKS
D MINOR

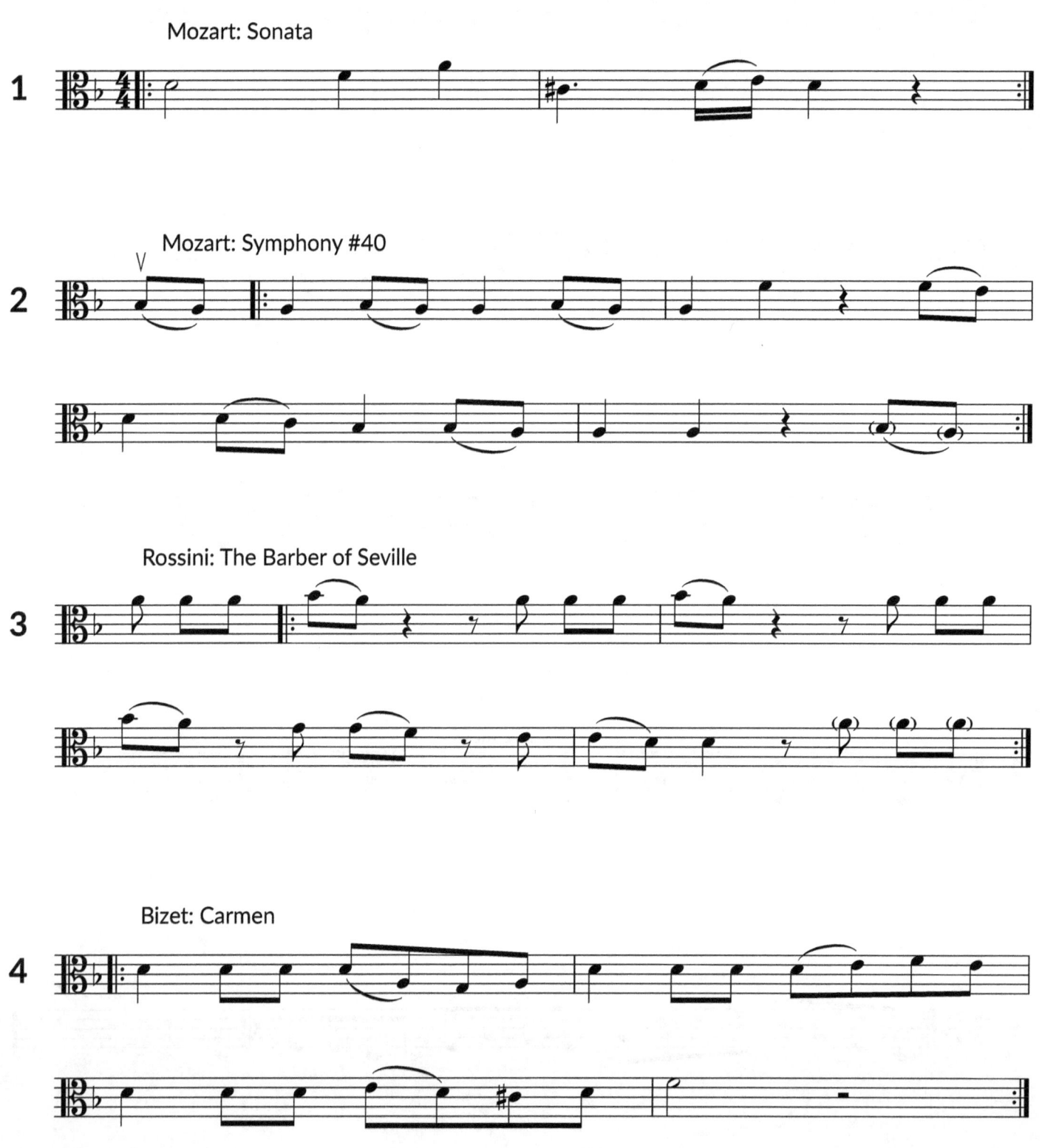

Mouret: Rondeau

Mozart: The Marriage of Figaro

Grieg: In the Hall of the Mountain King

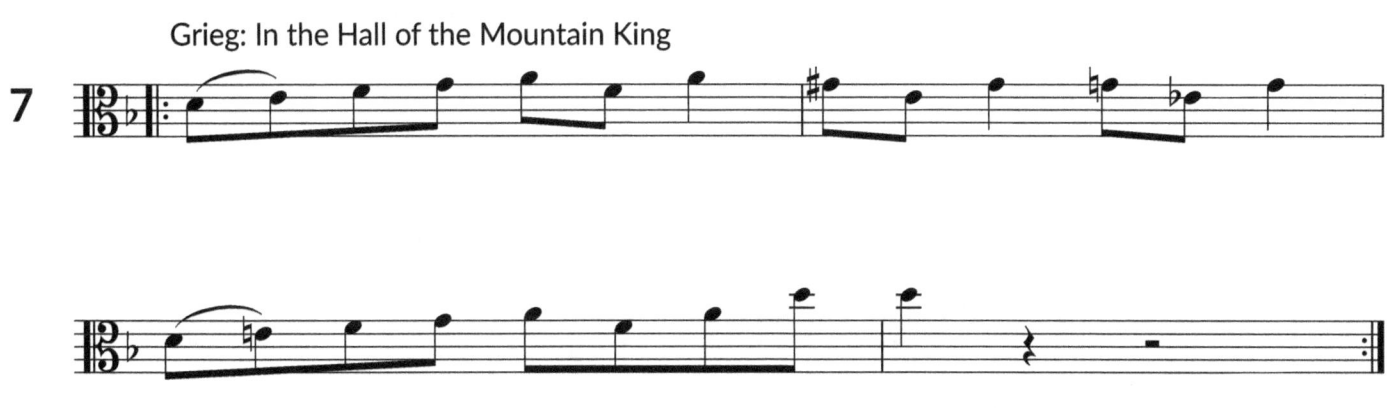

Bach: Little Fugue #1

Mozart: Eine Kleine

Bach: Little Fugue #2

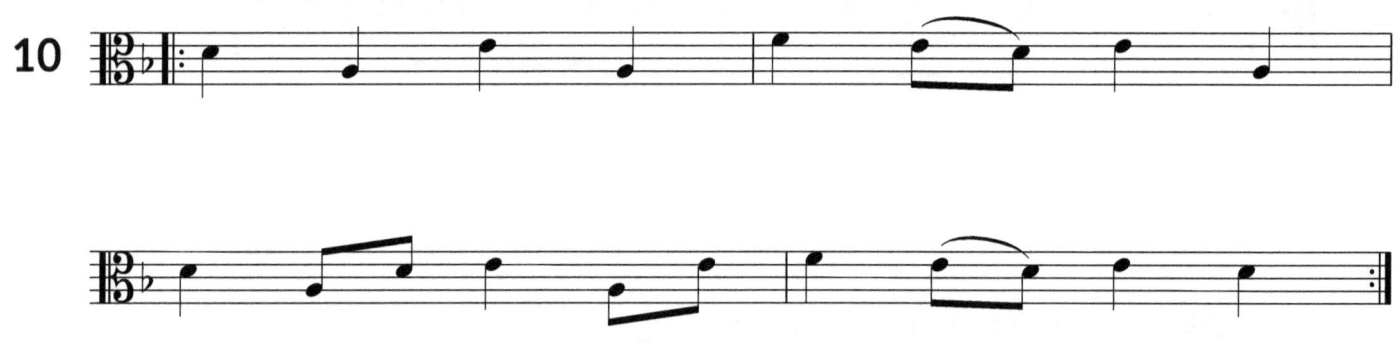

Bach: Suite #2

Tchaikovsky: 1812 Overture

13 Bizet: Carmen (Overture)

14 Bizet: Carmen (Habanera)

15 Bach: Jesu, Joy of Man's Desiring

16 Mozart: Rondo Alla Turca

©2025 Harry Hunt, Jr.

8th NOTE LICKS
D MINOR

1

2

3

4

5

6

7

8

9

10

16th NOTE LICKS
D MINOR

1

2

3

4

5

6

7

8

9

10

G MINOR

MELODIC MINOR SCALE
G MINOR

HARMONIC MINOR SCALE
G MINOR

ARPEGGIOS (QUARTERS)
G MINOR

1

2

3

4

ARPEGGIOS (8ths)
G MINOR

1

2

3

4

5

©2025 Harry Hunt, Jr.

POPULAR CLASSICAL LICKS
G MINOR

Mouret: Rondeau

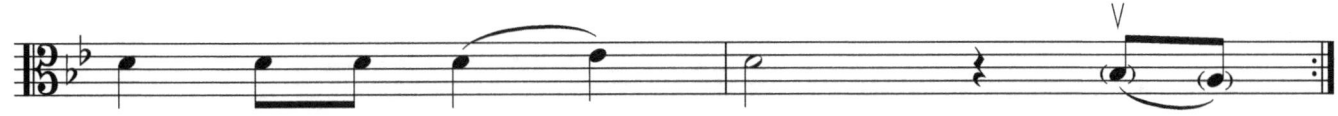

Mozart: The Marriage of Figaro

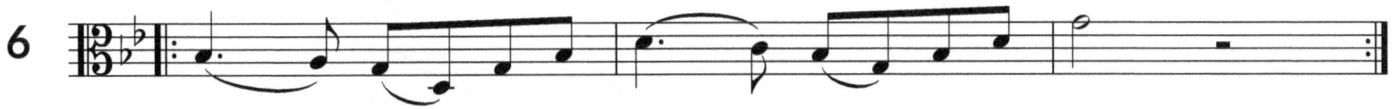

Grieg: In the Hall of the Mountain King

Bach: Little Fugue #1

©2025 Harry Hunt, Jr.

9 Mozart: Eine Kleine

10 Bach: Little Fugue #2

11 Bach: Suite #2

12 Tchaikovsky: 1812 Overture

Bizet: Carmen (Overture)

Bizet: Carmen (Habanera)

Bach: Jesu, Joy of Man's Desiring

Mozart: Rondo Alla Turca

©2025 Harry Hunt, Jr.

8th NOTE LICKS
G MINOR

1

2

3

4

5

16th NOTE LICKS
G MINOR

1

2

3

4

5

6

7

8

9

10

©2025 Harry Hunt, Jr.

C MINOR

MELODIC MINOR SCALE
C MINOR

HARMONIC MINOR SCALE
C MINOR

ARPEGGIOS (QUARTERS)
C MINOR

1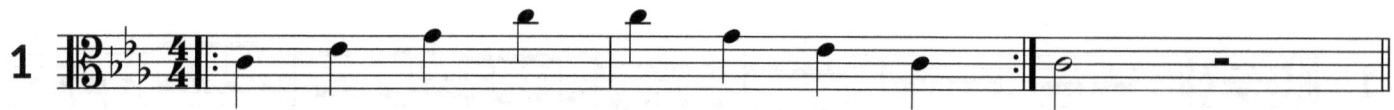

2

3

4

ARPEGGIOS (8ths)
C MINOR

1

2

3

4

5

POPULAR CLASSICAL LICKS
C MINOR

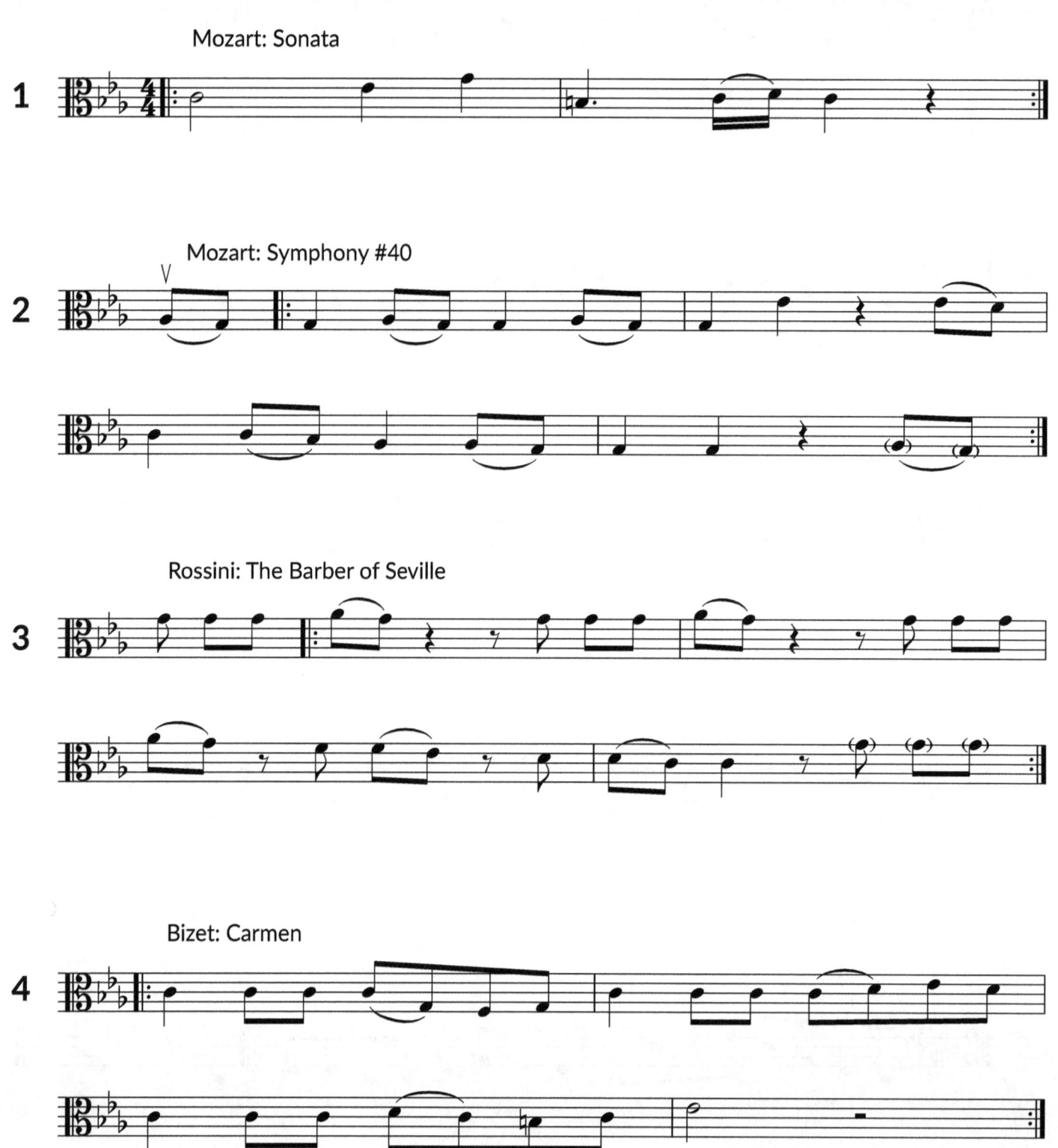

Mouret: Rondeau

Mozart: The Marriage of Figaro

Grieg: In the Hall of the Mountain King

Bach: Little Fugue #1

©2025 Harry Hunt, Jr.

Mozart: Eine Kleine

9

Bach: Little Fugue #2

10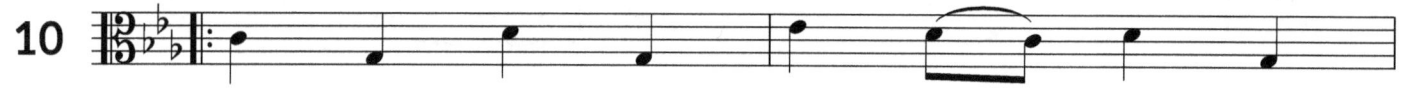

Bach: Suite #2

11

Tchaikovsky: 1812 Overture

12

Bizet: Carmen (Overture)

Bizet: Carmen (Habanera)

Bach: Jesu, Joy of Man's Desiring

Mozart: Rondo Alla Turca

8th NOTE LICKS
C MINOR

1

2

3

4

5

6

7

8

9

10

16th NOTE LICKS
C MINOR

1

2

3

4

5

6

7

8

9

10

www.ingramcontent.com/pod-product-compliance
Lightning Source LLC
LaVergne TN
LVHW061343060426
835512LV00016B/2649